DINOSAURS!

KU-031-500

TRICERATOPS
AND OTHER
HORNED HERBIVORES

by
David West

W
FRANKLIN WATTS
LONDON•SYDNEY

First published in the UK in 2013 by Franklin Watts

Franklin Watts
338 Euston Road
London NW1 3BH

Franklin Watts Australia
Level 17/207 Kent Street
Sydney, NSW 2000

All rights reserved.

Dewey classification: 567.9'158

A CIP catalogue record for this book is available from the British Library.

ISBN: 978 1 4451 2730 9

Franklin Watts is a division of Hachette Children's Books, an Hachette UK company.
www.hachette.co.uk

DINOSAURS! TRICERATOPS and other HORNED HERBIVORES
was produced for Franklin Watts by
David West Children's Books, 7 Princeton Court, 55 Felsham Road, London SW15 1AZ

Copyright © 2011 David West Children's Books

Designed and illustrated by David West

Printed in China

Contents

This is Triceratops. *It was one of the largest horned dinosaurs and is probably the best known (see pp.* 26–27).

SKIN

Like all dinosaurs, these giants had scaly, reptile-like skin. Some were studded with bony **nodules** along their sides. Some had spines running the length of their back from the neck to the end of the tail.

What Is a Horned **Herbivore**?

These were four-legged dinosaurs that lived mainly during the Upper Cretaceous period. They are known as **ceratopsids**. They looked like a rhinoceros, but they were generally much larger. They all had a neck frill, and many had horns, in various combinations, sticking out of their head and frill.

*Dinosaurs lived throughout the Mesozoic Era, which is divided into three periods, shown here. It is sometimes called the Age of the Reptiles. Dinosaurs first appeared in the Upper Triassic period and died out during a **mass extinction event** 65 million years ago.*

FRILL
The frill may have been used for defensive purposes. It may also have been used during courtship, turning colourful with bright markings.

HORNS
Most, but by no means all, of these dinosaurs had horns. Some, like *Triceratops*, had three horns growing from the head. Others had no horns but large **bosses** where horns might once have grown. Horns also grew from the neck frill, and spikes grew from the sides of the cheeks.

BEAK
All these ceratopsids had a parrot-like beak for tearing up tough plants. The animal then sliced the plants up with its **batteries** of teeth.

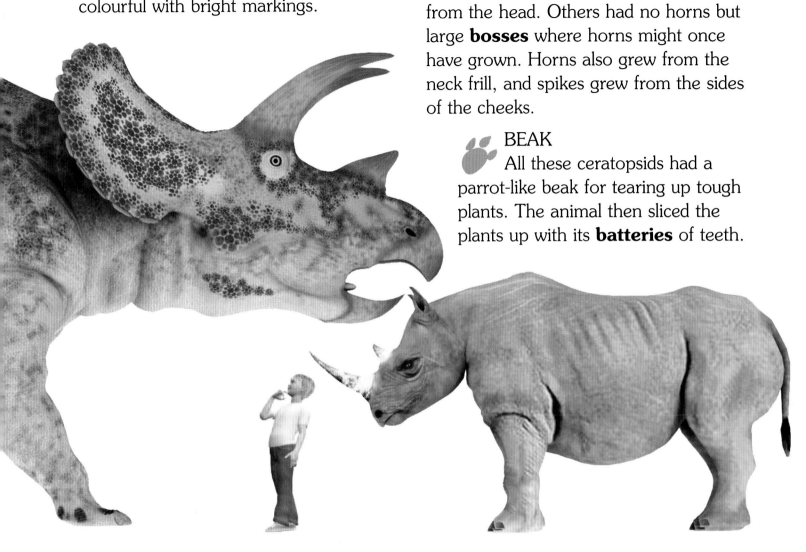

FOUR-LEGGED
These ceratopsids walked on four strong, sturdy legs. They had five toes on each of the front feet and four on each of the back feet. Each toe ended in a small hoof.

SIZE
Ceratopsids were generally the size of a family car. Some, like *Triceratops*, grew to 9 metres (30 feet) long. Others, like *Zuniceratops*, were only 3.4 metres (11 feet) long. A rhinoceros is about 3.4 metres (11 feet) in length.

	227	205	180	159	144		98		65 Millions of years ago (mya)
	Upper	Lower	Middle	Upper		Lower		Upper	
	TRIASSIC		JURASSIC				CRETACEOUS		

Upper Cretaceous
83–74 mya
United States

Achelousaurus

Achelousaurus is named after the ancient Greek river god Achelous. Achelous changed into a bull but had a horn torn off by the hero Heracles during a fight. The head of *Achelousaurus* has rough bosses over the eyes and nose, as if its horns have been torn away.

The skull of a full-grown *Achelousaurus*, including the frill horns, is over 1.5 m (5 feet) long. *Achelousaurus* has similarities with both *Einiosaurus* (see pp. 14–15), which has two horns at the end of the

A pair of Achelousauruses *face off during mating* **rituals** *in this scene from Upper Cretaceous North America. An* Achelousaurus *and an* Euoplocephalus *ignore them and feed on flowering plants while a tiny* Bambiraptor *tries to protect her nest.*

frill, and the hornless *Pachyrhinosaurus* (see pp. 16–17). The **fossil** bones of *Achelousaurus* were found in the same rock formation with, and therefore probably **co-existed** with, *Daspletosaurus, Bambiraptor, Euoplocephalus, Maiasaura* and *Einiosaurus*. *Achelousaurus* was a middle-sized ceratopsid. Males might have gathered together during the mating season to compete for mating rights.

Achelousaurus was about 6 metres (20 feet) long and weighed 3.6 metric tons (4 tons).

Chasmosaurus

Chasmosaurus was a type of ceratopsid dinosaur. Its name means 'opening lizard', referring to the large openings in its frill. Ceratopsids are split into two subfamilies: centrosaurids, which have short frills (like *Achelousaurus*), and chasmosaurids, which have long frills (like *Chasmosaurus*).

The long-frilled ceratopsids had longer faces, and some **paleontologists** think they were more selective about the plants they ate. Long frills

A large male Chasmosaurus *bellows out a call to keep the herd together during a heavy downpour in this scene from Upper Cretaceous North America. Fossil evidence suggests that these large dinosaurs may have lived in herds.*

were a late development in dinosaur **evolution**. The large frill of *Chasmosaurus* was heart-shaped – its structure consisted of two large loops of bone. The frill was large but flimsy, since it was mainly skin stretched between the bones. It would not have been used in defence. It is possible that it made the dinosaur appear large and frightening. It may also have had colourful markings.

Chasmosaurus was about 6 metres (20) long and weighed around 3.6 metric tons (4 tons).

9

Diabloceratops

Diabloceratops, meaning 'devil-horned face', is a recently discovered ceratopsid dinosaur. It was a typical ceratopsid, with a neck frill, spikes and horns. *Diabloceratops* had two large spikes on its neck frill, and a horn above each eye.

Unlike some other ceratopsids, *Diabloceratops* had no horn on its snout – a similar arrangement to *Diceratops* (see pp. 12–13). Its long frill might have had eye markings, which would confuse a **predator**

Bees buzz busily from flower to flower as a small group of Diabloceratopses *feed on flowering plants similar to modern-day magnolias in this scene from Upper Cretaceous North America.*

into thinking it was a much larger animal. The two large horns on top of the frill would also have made it look quite dangerous. Some experts have suggested that the frill may have been used as a way of **regulating** the body temperature. Blood vessels under the skin of the frill could have radiated heat away, keeping it cool, just as a radiator does in a car's engine.

Diabloceratops grew up to 6 metres (20 feet) long and weighed around 3.6 metric tons (4 tons).

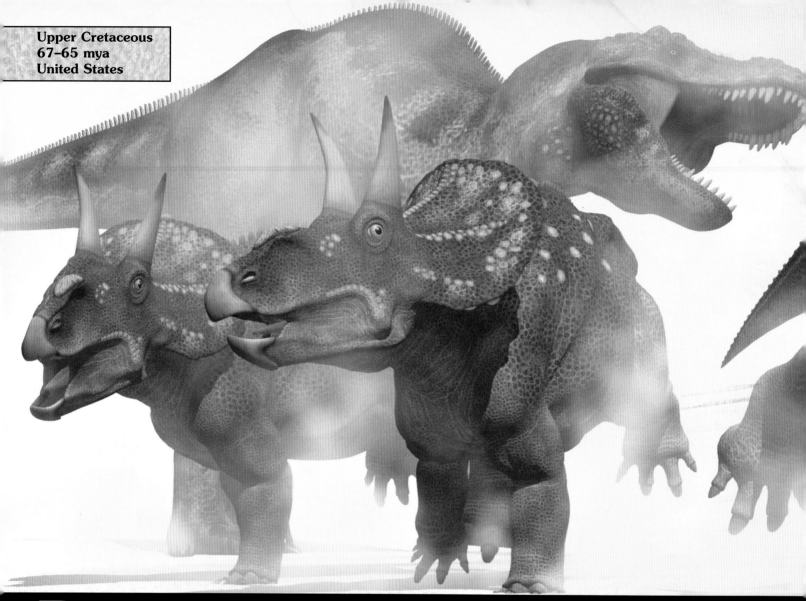

Diceratops

Diceratops, meaning 'two-horned face', is also known as *Nedoceratops*, meaning 'insufficient horned face', because of its lack of a nose horn. It was renamed *Nedoceratops* in 2007, when it was discovered that the name *Diceratops* was already being used for an insect.

Diceratops is known only from one poorly **preserved** fossil skull. On first inspection, it looks very similar to *Triceratops*, except that it has only two eyebrow horns and no nose horn. There is just a rounded

*A group of **inexperienced** young Diceratopses scatter before a hungry Tyrannosaurus rex in this scene from Upper Cretaceous North America. These four-legged dinosaurs would be better off standing their ground close together and using their horns for defence.*

stump where the nasal horn should be, and the eyebrow horns stand almost vertically. There are also holes in the frill, which were not found in *Triceratops* skulls. However, these may be due to damage done before or after the animal died. Little is known about *Diceratops*, but it is likely that it had a similar lifestyle to *Triceratops*. Its large beak was used to bite off tough plant stems and leaves from **cycads** and conifers.

Diceratops grew to 6 metres (20 feet) long and weighed over 4.5 metric tons (5 tons).

Einiosaurus

Einiosaurus, or 'bison lizard', is a medium-sized, short-frilled centrosaurid dinosaur. It is recognisable by its low, strongly forwards-curving nasal horn that looks like a bottle opener and by a pair of large spikes that point upwards from the relatively small frill.

Fossils of many *Einiosauruses* in **bone beds** are thought by experts to represent herds that may have died during a drought or flood. This suggests that *Einiosaurus*, like other centrosaurid dinosaurs such

14

A meat-eating Daspletosaurus *backs away from a herd of aggressive* Einiosauruses *who are protecting their young in this scene from Upper Cretaceous North America. These centrosaurids could defend themselves very effectively when they worked together.*

as *Pachyrhinosaurus* and *Centrosaurus*, lived in herds similar to modern-day animals such as bison or wildebeest. Dinosaurs that lived alongside *Einiosaurus* include hadrosaurids such as *Hypacrosaurus*, *Maiasaura* and *Prosaurolophus*; the **ankylosaurs** *Edmontonia* and *Euoplocephalus*; and the tyrannosaurid *Daspletosaurus* (which appears to have specialised in preying on ceratopsids such as *Einiosaurus*).

Einiosaurus grew up to 7.6 metres (25 feet) long and weighed up to 4.5 metric tons (5 tons).

Pachyrhinosaurus

Pachyrhinosaurus, meaning 'thick-nosed lizard',
was a centrosaurid dinosaur and closely related to
Achelousaurus. Like *Achelousaurus*, the skull did not
have horns, but instead had large, flattened bosses, the
largest being over the nose.

These flattened bosses were probably used in butting and shoving
matches during the mating season. As with other ceratopsids, their
neck frills may have been coloured to attract females.

16

While the herd grazes in the background, two male Pachyrhinosauruses *butt and shove in a show of strength. Undisturbed, a pair of* Maiasauras *continue to feed on ferns in the foreground in this scene from Upper Cretaceous North America.*

A single pair of curved, flattened horns grew from the top of the frill. Each fossilised skull found seems to have a different arrangement of frill horns. Some even had horns growing out of the central part of the frill. Fossil finds in bone beds have revealed large groups of adults with **juveniles**. This suggests that *Pachyrhinosauruses* looked after their young just as herding animals like bison and antelope do today.

Pachyrhinosaurus grew to 6 metres (20 feet) and weighed about 3.6 metric tons (4 tons).

Pentaceratops

Pentaceratops means 'five-horned face', which refers to the three horns on its head plus the two spikes that poke out of its cheeks. At 3 m (9.8 feet) long, its skull is the largest of all known land animals. It is closely related to *Chasmosaurus* (see pp. 8–9).

Fossil skulls were found in New Mexico along with the fossils of the different broad-leafed plants the animal ate. These plants looked like modern-day figs, willows, magnolias, and other types of hardwood

18

A large male Pentaceratops *drinks from a river while the rest of the herd feeds on the lush flowering hardwood plants. In the foreground, a group of young* Ornithomimus *chase newly hatched dragonflies along the riverbank.*

flowering plants. *Pentaceratops* lived in a landscape that was lush and full of these types of plant. As with all chasmosaurids, its large frill made this animal look bigger to its enemies than it actually was. Its long horns and imposing size when fully grown kept this dinosaur safe from predators. Only the young and sickly would be **vulnerable** to attack.

Pentaceratops was around 8.2 metres (27 feet) long and weighed about 5.4 metric tons (6 tons).

Protoceratops

Protoceratops, meaning 'first horned face', belonged to an early group of small ceratopsids known as protoceratopsids. Unlike later ceratopsids (such as *Triceratops*), it lacked horns and had holes in its frill.

Protoceratops's large neck frill may have protected the neck or been brightly coloured and used in courtship, or both. Large numbers of fossils of these dinosaurs have been found together, suggesting that they lived in herds. Paleontologists found that these dinosaurs lived in

In a scene from Upper Cretaceous Asia, a noisy Protoceratops *herd warms up in the early morning sun. Newly hatched youngsters scamper around as adults tend to their crude nests scooped from the desert sand.*

deserts. Large nest sites were discovered, where eggs were laid in shallow holes in the sand. Up to 12 or more eggs were laid in each nest. Small pores and the pattern on the shells show that the eggs were **adapted** for desert conditions. *Protoceratops* had a parrot-like beak, which it used to crop low vegetation. It had teeth behind its beak, which it used to mash the tough plants.

Protoceratops was about 1.8 metres (6 feet) long and weighed up to 409 kilogrammes (900 pounds).

Styracosaurus

Styracosaurus, 'spiked lizard', was a centrosaurid. It had six long horns and some smaller ones extending from its neck frill. It also had a small spike on each of its cheeks and a single horn up to 61 centimetres (2 feet) long protruding from its nose.

As with *Pachyrhinosaurus*, the neck frills of individual *Styracosauruses* varied. Some had small hook-like projections, others had only four large spikes, and some had the inner pair curving towards each other.

A group of Styracosauruses *make their way out of a valley during a drought in this scene from Upper Cretaceous North America. A* Styracosaurus *skull, lying in the foreground, shows the two large openings in the frill that are typical of most ceratopsids.*

Because of the position of its head, *Styracosaurus* probably fed mostly on low growth. The deep, narrow beak was used to rip and pluck at tough plants. Some scientists have suggested that ceratopsids like *Styracosaurus* ate palms and cycads, while others have suggested they ate ferns. They may have knocked down angiosperm trees and then **sheared** off leaves and twigs to eat.

Styracosaurus grew up to 5.5 metres (18 feet) long and weighed around 2.7 metric tons (3 tons).

23

Torosaurus

Torosaurus means 'perforated lizard', which refers to the holes in its long frill. It was a chasmosaurid dinosaur whose frilled skull reached 2.6 metres (8.5 feet) in length. It was very closely related to *Triceratops*, and some experts suggest it might even be a fully grown *Triceratops*.

Paleontologists think that young ceratopsid dinosaurs started life with a frill with no holes in it. As they got older, holes developed to keep the weight down. The holes would have been covered by stretched skin,

24

Bellowing and kicking up dust, a large male Torosaurus *chases off a younger, smaller male* Torosaurus *after a contest during courtship rituals in this scene from Upper Cretaceous North America.*

creating vivid eyespots when flushed with blood. These may have been used to frighten away predators or as a display during courtship rituals. Although fossil skulls have been found, very little is known about the rest of *Torosaurus*'s skeleton. The few pieces of skeleton that have been discovered show that it probably looked similar to other chasmosaurine ceratopsids such as *Pentaceratops*.

Torosaurus was about 7.6 metres (25 feet) long and weighed up to 6 metric tons (6.6 tons).

25

Triceratops

Triceratops, 'three-horned face', was one of the last dinosaurs to appear before the great mass extinction event. It shared the landscape with, and was preyed upon by, the fearsome predator *Tyrannosaurus rex*.

Although the horns and frill are seen as defensive weapons against predators, some experts suggest that they were used in courtship displays, like the antlers of modern reindeer. With the frill, its skull could grow to 2.1 metres (7 feet) in length. This would make

Adult male and female Triceratops *group together to fight off a* Tyrannosaurus rex *that is attempting to snatch a juvenile in this scene from Upper Cretaceous North America. The horn of the male* Triceratops *has caught the* Tyrannosaurus rex *in the neck.*

Triceratops seem much larger to a predator. Many fossil bones show damage from combat with rivals or predators. Although *Triceratops* is the best known of the ceratopsids, experts are still unsure of its position in the ceratopsid family. It has the short, solid frill of a centrosaurid and the long brow horns of a chasmosaurid. It is generally accepted to be a member of the chasmosaurid family.

Triceratops was about 9.1 metres (30 feet) long and weighed up to 11.8 metric tons (13 tons).

Zuniceratops

Zuniceratops, meaning 'Zuni-horned face', was a dinosaur that had many similar features to ceratopsids. However, it is thought by paleontologists to be an earlier type of dinosaur.

Zuniceratops lived about 10 million years earlier than the well-known ceratopsids and provides important information about how they evolved from the hornless protoceratopsids, like *Protoceratops*, to the later horned ceratopsids. Like *Protoceratops*, *Zuniceratops* was

28

A large herd of Zuniceratopses *run for their lives from a forest fire, started by a lightning strike or volcanic activity, in this scene from Upper Cretaceous North America. Volcanic eruptions were common during this period.*

smaller than later ceratopsids. It had a frill behind its head with holes in it, as later chasmosaurids did, but there were no horns or bones lining the edge of the frill. It is the earliest known dinosaur to have eyebrow horns, which are thought to have grown much larger with age. Like all other ceratopsids, it was four-legged and it was a herbivore.

Zuniceratops was 3.4 metres (11 feet) long and weighed up to 114 kilogrammes (250 pounds).

Animal Gallery

Other dinosaurs and animals that appear in the scenes.

Daspletosaurus (pp. 14–15)
'frightful lizard'
giant **carnivorous theropod**
Upper Cretaceous
Canada

Bambiraptor (pp. 6–7)
'baby raider'
dromaeosaurid (carnivorous bird-like theropod dinosaur)
Upper Cretaceous
United States

Euoplocephalus (pp. 6–7)
'well-armoured head'
ankylosaur (armoured herbivorous dinosaur)
Upper Cretaceous
Canada, United States

Ornithomimus (pp. 18–19)
'bird mimic'
omnivorous ornithomimosaur
Upper Cretaceous
Canada, United States

Maiasaura (pp. 16–17)
'caring mother lizard'
hadrosaur (duck-billed dinosaur)
Upper Cretaceous
United States

Tyrannosaurus rex (pp. 12–13)
'tyrant lizard king'
giant carnivorous theropod
Upper Cretaceous
Canada, United States

Glossary

adapted Changed to cope with a different condition or situation.

ankylosaur A member of the *Ankylosaurus* family of armoured dinosaurs.

batteries Rows or groupings in lines.

bone bed A layer of rock that contains bones or fossilised bones.

boss A body part that sticks out.

carnivorous Meat-eating.

ceratopsid A member of a beaked dinosaur family, such as *Triceratops*.

co-exist Live at the same time.

cycad A kind of palm.

dromaeosaurid A member of a group of carnivorous dinosaurs known as raptors, with slashing claws on their feet.

evolution Gradual change by natural selection over a long period of time.

fossil The remains of a living thing that have turned to rock.

hadrosaur A member of the family of duck-billed dinosaurs.

herbivore A plant eater.

inexperienced Having no knowledge of how to do something.

juvenile A youngster.

mass extinction event A large-scale disappearance of species of animals and plants in a relatively short period of time.

nodule A small, round lump, usually of hard skin or bone.

omnivorous Eating both plants and meat.

ornithomimosaur A theropod dinosaur that slightly resembled modern ostriches.

paleontologist A scientist who studies life forms from earlier geological periods by looking at fossils.

predator An animal that hunts and kills other animals for food.

preserved Kept from being destroyed.

regulate Adjust and control the amount of something, such as heat.

ritual A series of special acts or ways of doing something.

sheared Chopped, cut or cropped.

theropod A member of a two-legged dinosaur family that includes most of the giant carnivorous dinosaurs.

vulnerable Open to attack or injury.

Index